HOW TO DRY HERBS WITH EASE

A SUPERLATIVE GUIDE ON HOW TO DRY HERBS -: SPICES, CONDIMENTS & RECIPES

VIKKY GOLD

Table of Contents

CHAPTER ONE

INTRODUCTION
Drying Herbs

Preserving herbs in dried form is extremely mainstream since it is such a basic method to save them. Dried herbs can be utilized directly from their containers similarly as they are required for cooking or as trimming similarly as fresh herbs may be; be that as it may, the just-picked herb fragrance is lost in the drying procedure. Marjoram, mint, oregano, rosemary, and thyme dry well. A few people may like to freeze herbs, for example, basil, chervil, chives, cilantro (enormous level leafed and parsley-like), dill, and parsley in light of the fact that drying them might be disillusioning. See Freezing Fresh Herbs diagram connected at the head of this page.

Harvesting and drying

Herb leaves ought to be cut when the plant's load of fundamental oils is at its most elevated.

- In the verdant herbs (basil, chervil, marjoram, and exquisite) this happens not long before blooming time.

- Basil, lemon emollient, parsley, rosemary, and sage can be cut upwards of multiple times during the open air developing season.

Cutting ought to be done toward the beginning of the day of a day that vows to be hot and dry. When the dew is off the plants, cut off the main 6 crawls of stem beneath the blossom buds.

Drying in Bundle or bunches

Bundle drying is a simple method to dry since a long time ago stemmed herbs, for example, marjoram, savvy, exquisite, mint, parsley, basil, dill, and rosemary.

On the off chance that the leaves are perfect, it isn't important to wash them; a portion of the oils might be lost during flushing. In any case, if the leaves are dusty, or have been thickly mulched, flush them quickly under virus water. Shake off any abundance water and hang the herbs, tied in little packs, just until the water dissipates away. Dispose of any dead or yellowed leaves.

As quickly as time permits, take the herb bundles in and balance them in a warm, dry spot which is all around ventilated and not presented to coordinate daylight. (Generally, herbs were

Hung above kitchen chimney shelves or in storage rooms.)

Tie herbs and hang — verdant finishes down — with the goal that the fundamental oils in the stems will stream into the leaves. Try not to balance the herbs over the oven you cook on; oil and smells can harm the fragile surface, flavor, and fragrance of the herbs.

To keep dust from gathering on the drying leaves, place each pack inside a paper sack before hanging. Accumulate the head of the pack and tie the herb stems so the leaves hang uninhibitedly inside the sack. For ventilation, cut out the base of the pack or puncture the sides.

CHAPTER TWO

THERE ARE DIFFERENT APPROACHES TO DRY HERBS

- food dehydrator,

- tray drying

- microwave-stove drying.

Tray Drying

Plate drying functions admirably for seeds and huge leafed herbs. It is the most ideal decision for herbs with short stems that are hard to integrate for hanging. Dry the herbs on a shallow-rimmed plate secured with cheesecloth.

To dry leaves:

• Remove leaves from their stems or leave them joined.

• Spread just one layer of leaves on a plate to guarantee great air dissemination and speedy drying.

• Place the plate in a warm, dry, very much ventilated region that isn't presented to coordinate daylight.

• Every scarcely any days, mix or turn the leaves tenderly to guarantee in any event, drying. Contingent upon the temperature and mugginess, it takes around a week or so for herbs to dry totally.

•   When the leaves are fresh and altogether dry, expel them from the plate and store in a sealed shut holder.

To dry seeds

•   Spread seeds on plate in a slender layer.

•   Dry with respect to leaves. When dry, cautiously hands rub the seed cases and tenderly overwhelm waste. Store in a hermetically sealed container.

Microwave Drying

Microwaves can dry herbs rapidly. Be that as it may, outrageous alert ought to be utilized when microwave drying in light of the danger of searing the herbs as well as lighting a fire and harming the microwave.

•	If herbs should be washed, ensure all the abundance water is expelled; else, they will cook, not dry in the microwave.

•	Place close to 4 or 5 herb branches in the microwave, orchestrating them between 2 paper towels.

- Microwave on HIGH for 2 to 3 minutes; expel herbs from stove.

- If herbs are not fragile and dry, microwave on HIGH for an additional 30 seconds.

- Place herbs on a rack and let cool.

- Store in a water/air proof holder.

CHAPTER THREE

STEP BY STEP INSTRUCTIONS TO DRY HERBS

Of all the different kinds of foods and approaches to save them — freezing or canning leafy foods, pickling, relieving meat, making cheddar and yogurt — getting dried out herbs is the most effortless spot to bounce in. Most herbs contain so little dampness that your activity is done not long after you've purchased or reaped them.

Drying herbs is a financially adroit food conservation system, as well, in light of the fact that new and dried herbs and teas request significant expenses at the supermarket.

Your own dried herbs will taste better than locally acquired on the grounds that they'll be more up to date and consequently increasingly impactful. In the event that you develop your own herbs, you can likewise pick the most delicious assortments.

HERB DRYING BASICS

At the point when herbs are dried, they are protected from microscopic organisms, form and yeast, and will stay strong for at any rate six to a year. To expel dampness, all you need is air dissemination. Some glow can likewise help. The six strategies point by point here fit the bill.

Washing herbs as a rule isn't vital on the off chance that they are developed naturally. Collect herbs in early in the prior day recently created fundamental oils have been singed off by the sun, yet after the dew has dried. Expel old, dead, infected or shriveled leaves.

At the point when you collect herbs for their seeds, the seed heads ought to turn earthy colored and solidifying, however not yet prepared to break. To gather herbs for their blossoms

—, for example, chamomile blossoms or thyme spikes — clip bloom buds off the plants near the principal day the buds open.

Indoor Air Drying Herbs

Tie stems in packs and hang the herbs topsy turvy. Use bend ties so you can without much of a stretch fix the groups when stems shrivel as they dry. A warm, dry spot is ideal; maintain a strategic distance from the kitchen. Wrap muslin, a work produce pack or a paper sack with a few gaps around the group, and tie it at the neck.

A drying screen helps dry leaves or branches. Make your own

from an old window screen or equipment fabric work stapled to scrap wood or an image outline. Lay cheesecloth over the screen, and spot herbs on the fabric. Herbs can take a couple of hours to a few days to dry completely.

Sun based Drying Herbs

This strategy is simple on the off chance that you live in a warm, dry spot. The perfect sunlight based food-drying conditions are 100 degrees Fahrenheit and 60 percent moistness or less.

Utilize the sun's warmth to dry herbs; however don't open herbs to an excessive amount of direct daylight as this could make them dye. Sun oriented drying can be as low-tech as putting drying screens outside until your herbs are weak (get them around evening time). You can likewise dry herbs under the windshield or back window of your vehicle on a hot day. A DIY sun based food dryer with stackable drying screens, a glass top to trap radiation, a safeguard plate to transmit heat and a vent for air flow is helpful, as well.

Getting dried out Herbs with a Machine

Any apparatus that dependably turns out a decent item and sets aside you time and cash merits its expense. Food dehydrators go in cost from $30 to $400, with between $100 to $200 being the most ideal decision for the vast majority of us. Quality dehydrators have helpful highlights, for example, clocks and flexible temperature control. In the event that you keep the unit put away in a helpful spot, you'll use it all the more frequently and recover its expense in a season or two of basic food item reserve funds.

Dehydrators have a temperature control system — in a perfect world one you can modify — and a fan to course air. Round models with various stacking plate are the most vitality effective. Box-type models that permit you to evacuate a portion of the plate can be helpful for drying enormous things and can fill different needs, for example, sealing bread mixture or refined yogurt. Adhere to your machine's guidelines.

Stove Drying Herbs

Drying herbs in a stove sounds simple in light of the fact that the greater part of us have one and skill to utilize it. Be that as it may, this is really the most work concentrated, and the least vitality proficient strategy. Herbs should be dried at around 100 degrees, yet most broilers don't go that low. They likewise need air course, and a few broilers don't have vents. You'll have to get a broiler thermometer and trial. Give turning the stove a shot warm or its most reduced setting for some time, at that point turning it off (while leaving the light on). You can likewise take a stab at propping the entryway open somewhat with a wooden spoon.

Check to what extent it takes for the temperature to drop to 100 degrees and to what extent it remains at that temperature.

Herbs are far simpler than leafy foods to broiler dry since they dry all the more rapidly and are all the more sympathetic. On the off chance that you intend to figure out how to utilize your broiler for food parchedness, certainly start with herbs. Layer them on cheesecloth over a wire cooling rack to take into account air dissemination all around, and place the rack in the stove when the temperature is around 100 degrees.

Microwave Drying Herbs

The microwave can effectively dry herbs, yet note that food-drying specialists don't suggest it for drying nourishments that have more dampness. It's not as simple as air drying or utilizing an electric dehydrator.

To dry herbs in a microwave, peel leaves off of the stems and spot the leaves between layers of paper towels. Start on high force for 1 moment, permit a 30-second rest, and afterward switch back and forth between 30 seconds on high force and 30 seconds of rest. Most herbs should dry completely in a short time or less.

Cooler Drying Herbs

Another super-straightforward strategy for drying herbs fundamentally sums to disregard. Just stick them in the cooler and disregard them for a couple of days. This helpful hint was found by the late herb authority Madalene Hill and her little girl, Gwen Barclay, who added to MOTHER EARTH NEWS 20 years back.

Coincidentally, they found that herbs took off alone (out of bundling) in a cool, dry fridge dried perfectly fresh and furthermore held their shading, flavor and scent.

They even loved this technique for parsley and chives, which don't have gained notoriety for keeping incredible flavor in dried structure. The test is discovering sufficient space to let herbs sit revealed for a couple of days.

On the off chance that your ice chest has accessible space, definitely, check out it.

Putting away Home-Dried Herbs

Your herbs have got done with drying when you can disintegrate them effectively, however don't disintegrate them all! Entire leaves and seeds hold oils preferred away over disintegrated herbs. In any case, having some pre-blended zest mixes —, for example, those for Italian, Mexican or grill dishes — can be a major life hack. Utilize a mortar and pestle to granulate the fixings. Tea mixes are additionally valuable, for example, a mix of peppermint and fennel to quiet a steamed stomach. Store dried herbs in sealed shut containers out of direct light and away from high warmth.

Continuously name jolts quickly with the date and substance. In the event that you grew a specific assortment, make certain to incorporate its name so you can pinpoint your top choices after some time. Check new containers for beads of dampness or form. Toss out anything mildew covered, and redry anything that made dampness in the container.

When utilizing dried herbs in plans that call for new, remember that oils in dried herbs are progressively thought. Use about a large portion of the measure of dried herbs in a formula calling for new herbs, and about a quarter so a lot if the dried herb has been finely ground. To utilize herbs in teas, pour bubbling water over a teaspoon to a tablespoon of the dried herb, or more to taste, and steep for 5 to 10 minutes.

Picking Herbs for Drying

The accompanying herbs are acceptable possibility for drying. A few herbs, in spite of the fact that they can be dried, hold their flavor better whenever solidified. These incorporate basil, borage, chives, cilantro, lemongrass, mint, parsley.

Leaves: straight, celery, chervil, dill, geranium, lemon salve, lemon verbena, lovage, marjoram, oregano, rosemary, sage, summer appetizing, tarragon, thyme

Seeds: anise, caraway, celery, chervil, coriander, cumin, dill, fennel, mustard

Blossoms: honey bee analgesic, chamomile, chive, dill, geranium, lavender, linden, marigold, nasturtium, rose, thyme, yarrow

CHAPTER FOUR

HEALTH BENEFITS OF HERBS

Herbs have been utilized since old occasions for their restorative properties, for the most part gathered into teas and colors. All the more as of late, their empowering an incentive as a food fixing has been figured it out. For one, herbs add an explosion of flavor to food, permitting you to curtail salt without yielding taste. What's more, a few herbs, including parsley, have huge measures of the basic nutrients A, C and K.

In any case, the genuine influence of herbs lies in their abundance of defensive polyphenols — plant mixes with intense cancer prevention agent and calming impacts. Heaps of studies show that polyphenols in herbs help battle such sicknesses as malignant growth, coronary illness, Alzheimer's, diabetes and that's just the beginning. Polyphenols are against microbial, so they can help shield us from unsafe microorganisms too. Albeit a considerable lot of the investigations on herbs' belongings have included concentrated arrangements of the leaves' dynamic segments, there is proof that their advantages despite everything apply when they are cooked and eaten as a major aspect of a normal dinner, as well.

Purchasing and putting away

The most ideal approach to have new herbs readily available is to develop them yourself, in your nursery or in pots on your windowsill. Along these lines, you should simply cut as wanted, and the magnificence and aroma of the plants will be a characteristic suggestion to utilize them.

When purchasing cut herbs, ensure the leaves are not shriveled or yellowing — they ought to be brilliant or dark green, contingent upon the assortment, and peppy looking. To store them, wash and pat or turn dry in a serving of mixed greens spinner, at that point envelop them by a sodden paper towel and spot in a plastic sack or a hermetically sealed compartment.

Notwithstanding how cautiously you choose or refrigerate them, new cut herbs are exceptionally transitory. The tenderest leaves, for example, basil and cilantro, will as a rule not last over seven days in the fridge. Firmer sorts, for example, parsley and oregano will keep somewhat more, and healthy rosemary and thyme will last two or three weeks. To safeguard them longer, hack them and spot in ice shape plate with stock or water. Freeze; at that point move the herb 3D squares into a plastic pack and keep solidified to add to soups, stews and sauces.

Some herbs offer a spotless, splendid flavor and spring like intrigue, don't discount dried, which have upsides of their own. Dried herbs are anything but difficult to keep close by, and they are in any event as gainful as new, if not more thus, on the grounds that the drying procedure really thinks the polyphones and flavors. When purchasing dried herbs, get them in little amounts that you can go through in under a year, in light of the fact that their flavor blurs with time. Furthermore, remember that, when in doubt, if a formula calls for one tablespoon of a new slashed herb, you can commonly substitute one teaspoon dried.

A STEP BY STEP GUIDE TO DRYING YOUR Favorite HERBS

A Step-by-Step While most herbs are appropriate for drying, some are simpler to dry than others. Herbs with low dampness content, for example, straight leaves, oregano, rosemary and thyme, dry quite well. Those with more slender, bigger leaves, for example, basil, parsley and sage, likewise take well to drying yet should be dried all the more rapidly to keep shape from framing on the leaves.

Harvesting and Prepping

1. Reap herbs before they blossom, as they will in general lose a portion of their flavor and can even be somewhat unpleasant once they have bloomed.

2. Pick herbs toward the beginning of the day, which is the point at which the oil substance of their leaves is most noteworthy and the flavor is at its pinnacle.

3. Wash the leaves if necessary to evacuate soil or residue, and take out any stained foliage. Delicately dry the herbs utilizing a dishcloth or paper towels.

4. Tie herbs into packs. For herbs with more dampness in the leaves, similar to basil and parsley, limit the packs to four to six stems to permit them to dry quicker. On the off chance that you live in a muggy atmosphere, make the groups littler to advance drying.

Utilize elastic groups, twine, or turn connections to integrate the herbs at the base of their stems. Ensure the tie is genuinely close, as the stems will contract as the herbs dry.

Drying the Herbs

Select an indoor area with great air flow. Evade any regions where the sun will sparkle on the herbs, as this can diminish their flavor and blanch the leaves. You have a couple drying alternatives once you have collected and prepared your herbs.

Alternative 1: Hang the packs topsy turvy. You can connect them to a coat holder, a drying rack or a stepping stool, or balance them from the roof utilizing twine or string.

Alternate 2: Punch 10 gaps in an earthy colored paper lunch sack and spot the herb packages topsy turvy in it — be mindful so as not to stuff them. Tie the sack shut and balance it from a help as depicted in the past model. This strategy is helpful for increasingly sticky locales where herbs may take more time to dry. The sack shields the herbs from dust and will get any stems that sneak out.

Alternate 3: Place the herbs in a solitary layer on a screen, in a similar area with respect to the past alternatives. You can put the screen on a table or up on blocks to all the more likely empower wind current, as that will permit the herbs to dry on the two sides. At regular intervals, give the herbs to help advance in any event, drying.

Alternate 4: You can broiler dry them for brisk outcomes, yet this will bring about somewhat less flavor than if you permit them to dry normally. Set the temperature to 100 degrees Fahrenheit and leave the broiler entryway open. Spot the herbs on a preparing sheet and put into the stove, making a point to even now leave the entryway open. Turn the herbs like clockwork until they will be they are dry, and evacuate.

Alternate 5: If you have a dehydrator, you can without much of stretch dry herbs in a generally short measure of time.

On the off chance that you've chosen to dry your herbs normally, start checking them following seven days. The length of drying time can go from as meager as a couple of days to a month, contingent upon the mugginess and strategy for drying. When the leaves are dry and firm, they are prepared.

SOME DRIED HERBS EVERY COOK SHOULD HAVE

Dried herbs can't be beaten for comfort or worth. They can energize any dish and take it from dull and exhausting to amazingly heavenly in only one sprinkle. Here and there it tends to be dubious to know which herbs to coordinate with what dishes and flavors, so we've accomplished the difficult work for you. In case you're hoping to tidy up a stew or pep up your pasta, look no further...

Some valuable tips

Purchasing and preserving

• Light and warmth are the adversaries of dried herbs and flavors, so don't keep them in a rack close to the oven. A plastic box is perfect - stick a mark on each container top, so it's anything but difficult to peruse from above.

• We like Seasoned Pioneers, which bundles herbs and flavors in resealable foil sachets - they keep going for a long time.

• If you're searching for something unique, steenbergs.co.uk offers a worldwide scope of to a great extent natural herbs and flavors.

Its site is pressed with know-how and plans motivation.

• Specialist and discount shops offer goliath packs at low costs, yet for the normal family it's more astute to purchase in little amounts all the more regularly.

• The Bart run (bart-ingredients.co.uk) has containers with flip tops, permitting you to spoon or sprinkle.

Getting the best structure your herbs

• In a formula, 1 tsp dried herbs rises to 1 tbsp new. By and large, utilize 1/4 - 1/2 of dried herbs for each serving.

•	To discharge flavor, dried herbs are best rehydrated. Include either toward the start of cooking, or around 20 minutes before the end. Take a stab at blending herbs in with 1 tsp of oil and leaving for 10-15 minutes before utilizing in dressings, marinages or sauces. Rather than sprinkling dried oregano on a pizza, steep in a little oil and use as a shower.

•	Dried herbs are a valuable method to eliminate salt. Where conceivable, include them during cooking instead of sprinkling on top.

Dry your own

•	Put sage, rosemary, thyme, oregano, mint or marjoram leaves in a solitary layer between sheets of kitchen paper and microwave on high for 1-2 mins until weak.

•	If you have a narrows tree, utilize the leaves new, or air-fry by balancing stems in a breezy spot, at that point taking out leaves to store in a tin or container.

The fundamentals

Rose petals

Rose petals likewise make delightful cake and cupcake adornments.

Dill

Dried dill is helpful where new isn't accessible, to give a Scandinacian contact to fish, egg dishes and potatoes (don't mistake for dill seeds, which are utilized in pickles).

Oregano

Oregano is the one herb that is commonly viewed as preferable dried over new. It's vital in Italian and Mexican cooking, particularly with tomatoes and cheddar. Its cousin marjoram is frequently neglected, however offers a better, less confident flavor, helpful for red meats and heartbeats.

Bay leaves

A few narrows leaves will give smooth pleasantness to braises, stews, stocks and soups. A narrows leaf alos rolls out a satisfying improvement when seasoning custards and rice puddings - mix warmed milk, or mix in with the rice.

Thyme

Dried thyme is a multi-reason herb to fly into a soup or goulash when a twig of new isn't accessible. Likewise incredible with chicken.

Lavendar

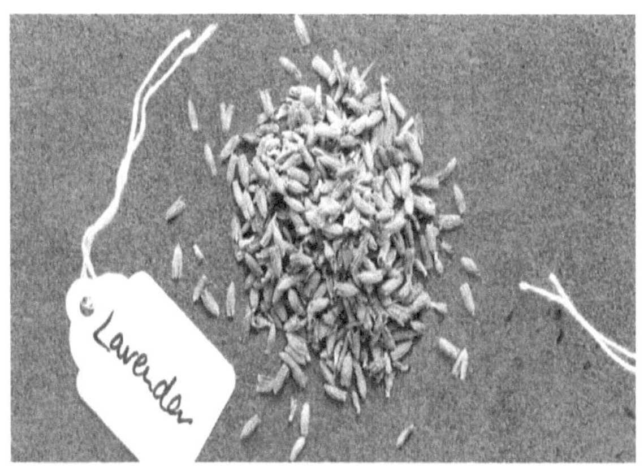

Lavendar is acceptable in shortbread or as an enhancing for frozen yogurt or custard. Sprinkle sparingly onto sheep or slick fish before simmering or preparing.

Sage

Scoured (or disintegrated) sage is superior to powdered. It comes up short on the punch of new, however it supplements poultry, pork and butternut squash and stuffings.

Lime leaves

Some of the time called kaffir lime leaves, tear or shred into Thai soups and curries for a particular citrus flavor.

Rosemary

Rosemary adds a pine scent to slow-ccoked dishes (especially Italian-style soups, stews, braises and all sheep dishes). Use sparingly, and slash on the off chance that you don't need spiky leaves in your completed dish.

Mint

Mint has made an ongoing rebound, because of the pattern for Middle Eastern food. Like new, dried mint can overwhelm, so use sparingly. Spearmint is increasingly fit to exquisite dishes (particularly Greek dishes, sheep and split pea soup) than peppermint (use for desserts and chocolates).

Lemongrass

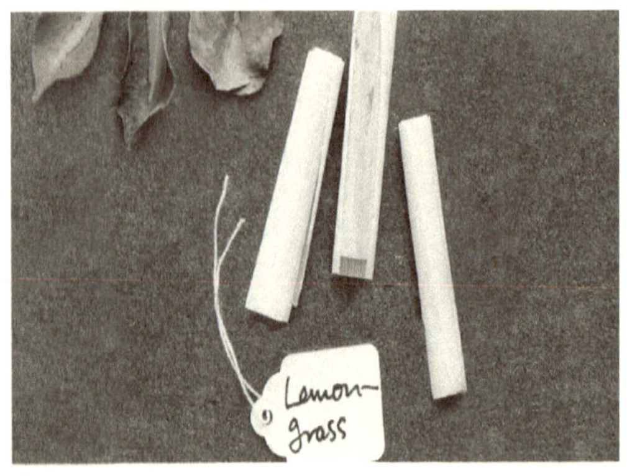

Pick freeze-dried lemongrass stalks, which have nearly a similar splendor and scent as new. Alongside lime leaves - additionally best freeze-dried-lemongrass is acceptable in curries and Thai dishes including coconut.

THE END